THE MOUTHS
of GRAZING
THINGS

The Brittingham Prize in Poetry

THE MOUTHS
of GRAZING
THINGS

Jennifer Boyden

THE UNIVERSITY OF WISCONSIN PRESS

The University of Wisconsin Press
1930 Monroe Street, 3rd Floor
Madison, Wisconsin 53711-2059
uwpress.wisc.edu

3 Henrietta Street
London WC2E 8LU, England
eurospanbookstore.com

5   4   3   2   1

Printed in the United States of America

Library of Congress Cataloging-in-Publication Data

Boyden, Jennifer.
    The mouths of grazing things / Jennifer Boyden.
        p. cm. — (Brittingham prize in poetry)
    Poems.
    ISBN 978-0-299-23514-7 (pbk. : alk. paper)
ISBN 978-0-299-23513-0 (e-book)
    I. Title. II. Series: Brittingham prize in poetry (Series)
PS3602.09344M68   2010
813'.6—dc22
2009039720

For Ian & Gavia

Contents

3.

Acknowledgments

Grateful acknowledgment is made to the editors of publications in which some of the poems from this collection, sometimes in different versions, first appeared:

Blue Violin: "The Pardon"
Cimarron Review: "Fly Tier's Monomania"
Cincinnati Review: "I'd Have Presented a Cup of Water or My Own Small Ax"
Clackamas Literary Review: "Covetous" and "Something to Go By"
Cold Mountain Review: "Gravity"
Georgetown Review: "What the Ghost Knows"
Inkwell: "Out of the Barn"
The Journal: "Asked Some 20 Questions, Many of Which Seem Like More Than One," "Seizure on the Siskyou Ridge," and "Will There
Be Police"
North Dakota Quarterly: "Potential: Two Times"
Paris Review: "Substitute"
Ploughshares: "Vandals"
Poetry East: "Plenty Comes at Night"
Poetry Northwest: "Running the Bulls"
Poets Against War: "Laying Them Down, Telling Them Rest"
Red Rock Review: "Floating Even Now" and "The Moss"
The Sow's Ear Poetry Review: "As Walking Becomes the Answer to the Road"
Sycamore Review: "Making It Big, Standing Back to Be Sure"
Virginia Quarterly Review: "Orectic" and "The Listener"
West Branch: "I Wonder if I've Told You Everything," "A Pileup, and Time, Besides," "Churn," and "What the Stones Allow"
Willow Review: "Twin"
Willow Springs: "The Allocations of Sound" and "Flag"

Poems from this book were also published in *Evidence of Night* and *Twenty Views of Cascade Head*, both limited-edition artist books by Crab Quill Press, Walla Walla, Washington.

It is a privilege to thank Nance Van Winckel for the longtime generosity of ideas and self; my parents, Thomas and Connie Oakes, for being generally amazing; Linda Andrews, Irvin Hashimoto, and Daniel Lamberton for thoughtful readership. Thanks also to John Bisbee, Jessica Henricksen, and Tracy Sitterley for seeing in ways that make things happen; to the PEN Northwest Margery Davis Boyden Wilderness Writing Residency; and to the Washington State Artist Trust for the gifts of time and place. Finally, my heart and gratitude to my husband and daughter, who wake up early and begin to make.

still I said as if to the alien in myself
  I do not speak to the wind now:
for having been brought this far by nature I have been
brought out of nature
and nothing shows me the image of myself

—A. R. AMMONS

1.

The Listener

I begin each day blank as an uncut key,
but in the shower I start hearing
neighbors twelve blocks over
washing the body of their mother.

It comes through the pipes, comes tight
as the lasso of a stutter, dragging
its words from the tongue's falling house.
Then, the advice of psychics

when I pick up my telephone, eight thousand
voices, all asking if they must eat
alone at the table
of their hearts forever. I hear

the mannequins shamed by their frozen wrists;
the shot star calling out to the dust
of old planets that it is coming;
trees unbinding storms from their branches.

But hardest to hear are the seeds of the bloodfruit—
words so red they enter
only at knifepoint. They believe
they are alone in their cardinal tongue,

sanguine and praying. It would take fire or breaking
glass to tell them the poppy, the apple, and the vein.

Orectic

From the throats of heron and lost wolves,
we learn of a mistake made by the gods.
They gave us red-winged birds and vesper
sparrows who make songs of leaf-light
and flying. The gods thought we'd be so happy—
all that fruit, one big garden,
our nakedness in sun and water.
They never counted on our needing a sound
for longing, too. They gave that to the loon,
to wild dogs whose teeth throb
from the light of the moon; they poured it
into the long necks of birds. How could they
have known? Where in our bodies
would they have moored the slender cry of the crane
who calls out that night is closing the sky,
taking away the glinted green
of the frogs' moist backs, the dazzle the sun makes
of every hair, of every shining wing?

What the Ghost Knows

Your ghost has spent so long neither dead
nor undead that it knows little, but wants to please you
with its learning. *Is this good?* it asks, pickling
a cat's tail or shoving pens through the mattress.
You are busy, but have time to shake your head. *Not that,*
you say, *this,* and show it.
You arrive home, see the ghost was bent on learning
without you: *This? This? That?* It points
to bottles glued to the rug, a chimney
full of corn, the neighbor's head
in a chair. *No,* you say, *like this.*
You ask the ghost to stop trying, suggest it
experiments with a very short piece of string.
But the ghost is interested in your world of matter,
its medium, material: much
can go wrong with a spoon, latex on the heater, scissors
in the car. But the ghost is learning.
The ghost wants to know
why so few things go together, how it happened
so much got severed from so much else,
combs your hair with a fork while it asks.

Covetous

Inside the jar, the brain swirled
and almost thought: *I float.*
Or some days, nearly this: *Magnificent?*
I am gray and—
hovering, . . . something, fills me? However,

the man who believed in the brain
said it understood, said that,
sprung from its body, it was gone so far
it no longer needed
the compass, the wheel, or the knife.
Each day,

to keep the brain from going
too far beyond himself, he placed
an apple in front of it.

You old convolution, he'd whisper,
you gray heart, you
translator of what is red and sweet.

Running the Bulls

We were not to tell our mother of summer
in the bull pasture. Whoever won
the fight to be sick got to lie alone with her
so she could tell about her days before
her heart got dizzy.

We were seven children, lonely each
in our small parts of the whole. Winters, we jumped
rooftops to snowdrifts, praying
for just one broken arm.
Nothing.

We had to make the bulls
hate us. When they fell lock-kneed
into sleep, dumb with the size of themselves,
we'd thistle-whip some into waking. Sparks
from their eyes caught, then lit. We ran.

Each hoof carried the weight
of the herd as the earth threw us forward
fast, the fence beyond
or under the dust. Behind, their breath,
frothed and hot on our backs.

Six more steps: maybe we'd see
a brother thrown up and over,
his hair like a banner and his hands
on his ass; perhaps a sister, clearing it,
barely. Whatever the end,

it was pain enough to make it.
We took turns holding each other
to our chests to hear our hearts slam against
whatever walls we had to have between us.
Then we'd watch through the fence slats

where the bulls began to fight themselves
just for the blood of it.

Relying on What I Know of How the Hidden Feels, I Advance a Theory

I showed God the pool of fish because
he said no one thought he had a sense of humor. *Look,*

I said, *these are funny—flashy*
kissers, the silver darts of them. God nodded, but said
he'd meant for them to rule the world. *But then evolution,*
he said, *and, you know, it just didn't work.*

Carrots, I said. *Now those are funny.*
God said they were close and he could see my point,
but they just weren't enough of what he meant.
Then I remembered something

and tilted back my head so he would watch me swallow.
Excellent! said God. *I'd forgotten all about that one.*

He said at first he'd put little apples everywhere: into the legs
of crickets and on the beaks of grackles.
We decided he'd been right
to take them out because they lacked subtlety. I was glad

he kept them in the bodies
of trees and stones and lined our backs with them, thrown them
into us
as if they were the coals by which we might burn.

Flag

It turned out I was there for the anthem,
not the cowboys, their hard smiles
and dinner-plate buckles sending back the sun.

Somewhere between dawn's early light
and the ramparts, the horse
galloped by, its wake filling

with the turquoised voice of the anthem.
The horse dragged the song like a flag
until it overlapped at the edges

and burst open wide. Then everything got smeared
with America. Every horse that bucked
under that strap and every rider who fell or made it

became the country. Clowns came out
and then bulls and ropes and chaps, spurs,
hats, calluses, and boots. The announcer saying

we sat at the edge of the most dangerous
playground in the world. All its players grew up
with one fist forever fisted and the other

full of sugar just in case something pretty
with its head held high came along and needed
to be broken one way or the other.

Vandals

They wrote it all down for me
in the living room on the walls.
They wrote who gave it up and who wanted it
most and a phone number. They told me
where to stick it, how to like it,
what the consistency was. There was a lot
I didn't get, but they left more under the bridge
and against the back of Red Plank Records.
I never met them. They'd come in the smoke
of my absence, during the hum
of appliances that needed to be wrapped
with stuffing and tape.
They made me the queen of their intent,
all the messages like stars
on the undersides of overpasses. I stay informed
about the people—what they do to each other,
how to take it, what number to call
for a piece of your own, and what happens
if you're not there to get it.
I watch for them to come back.
I watch for them from across the street
in my rented room with the walls painted red
and my little bit on and the curtains
more than slightly parted.

Out of the Barn

We climbed the lofts to reach the rafters
and waited for someone to throw the rope.
We'd sit on the knot and fall thirty feet
before the rope caught
and swung us. Once, the neighbor kid forgot to hang on
but said he loved the fall
right down to the smack
of body on the pile of hay. He began climbing
trees or lofts just to jump out of them.
He said he was training the world to catch him.
His sister still blames us,
but even after the funeral, she crept through the pasture
and into the loft.
She untied her braids and teased out her thin hair
to look like a woman ravaged.
She sailed through
the barn's wide doors
and then back in. When the rope snapped from its beam,
she kept going, clinging
to that rope as it trailed the air behind her—over cattle troughs
and fences, through the branches of an oak.
Her hair slipped from its tangles and,
between the strips of sun
and shadow, shone.

Something to Go By

In the morgue, they're searching for a scar
to become her name.

But no tattoos, no burns, nothing
to call her by. One of them saying
to the other, *Oh*
god, not another mute.

What she needs is a story
told by the flesh so someone can show up
and claim it.

It is not good to have been
perfect. It is not enough
to have loved the birds most

when they sang so darkly it almost wasn't green
anymore.

Mercy, to have pushed her down the stairs
or thrown the knife that scarred.
Anything to get her home.

Substitute

He asked for tighter guts, for more
and thicker hair: what he could have been
if Brooklyn hadn't held a gun to his head
for a token. No magazine wants
the fantasies I make of him. He's a farmer,
Brooklyn erased

to make this work. There, never the not-nothing
of a chicken's neck snapping in his hands, never
a cow turning the earth hollow with its dead drop
into the mouth of the family who shot and ate it.
I give him to the earth.

Of his hands I make great
and sturdy things. They turn soil, bring stumps up
from deep. He knows the knives I keep
in my barn by their fit against his palm, trusts
how they sharpen into what must be taken
down the middle. My fences
keep his day beasts safe; his wind blinds do not fail.

Should he wake to check the gates,
he'll return to find me watching: I built him
of what made me—first the lakes of Minnesota,
black depths frozen or a silver spear of fish;
then the hand that holds the hammer and the one that brings
the horses into calm.

I work on what he wants or wants erased—
the hands' touch gone blind from callus,
the hat's brown band of sweat. Even the horse
that will buck him hard and far if not
for the liquid ride of his body which into him I pour.

Twin

The boy whose stomach filled
with a tumor was cut open and healed.
They didn't show him
what they took: the twin
of his own split cell. Eight teeth, black hair,
face bound like a fist. At first
the boy felt better, then
without:

His second heart no longer told him
how to live. His second teeth

no longer demanded their meat. A long
time after, the boy heard the hidden thoughts
of strangers, answers
to where the twin had been. He didn't meet
a woman who also heard this way.
But in the story where he does,
she says, *Each of us has two hearts*
even when there is only one.

Regret

I am sawing again through
the storm's fallen trees.
The chainsaw grip and roar
speak to the spinning whetstone
inside me. They converse
until something demands
to be oiled. Deeper in my body,
a little knife
sharpens itself and prepares. *So sharp*,
it says, *nearly ready*. Soon
it will ask me to feel it.

Potential: Two Times

1.

After the dogs speak, they watch
for what to do next. We hold up
our arms, and they stand on two legs.
We snap twice, and they get in line.

Every year brings us one more dog.
You tell us you like the one with a scar
for a tail. He tears himself in his sleep,
swallowing his own skin and fur.

He wakes us with howls that startle
like grouse into air.
In our third year, we found him, taught him
how to sit, lie, beg.

In the sixth year, we talked
about how much longer our time could be
like this—taking dogs out of pity or hope
that maybe this one or that might blanket

the space between TV and sleep. There's only
so much that dogs care to know. The fourth
can put laundry in the washer, and the second
will open doors before us. But they prefer

the first commands we gave them:
Come here, come up, come back. Stay.

2.

You asked us if you could have the dog
with no tail. He was alone for so long
he forgot he had a body, and you need him.

When you hold him, he presses every part
of himself into you. He remembers
his body only when it is touched.

Surely this means something to you—
knowing he rips his flesh to make sure
it is there. He takes it into his teeth

and grows ravenous with touch. Every time
you return to him, you think of ways
to never leave again. Come here, you say,

stay. Finally it is too much, so you ask
what to do. We tell you to buy a bird
and we'll train it to ride the back of the dog.

We'll teach it every word we know, though
it only needs those first commands
and to be just enough weight to matter.

Making It Big,
Standing Back to Be Sure

Spraying the lacquer was a crime
and we knew it, but we were making
something big and it had to shine.
We sprayed late at night; in the morning,
children walking by for school fainted
into the grass. Frogs blistered in their pools,
which hurt us, too, but what we made was almost done.
We pushed open the doors and rolled it into the lawn.
The drivers-by pumped their brakes,
collided anyway, and lay wrecked, but still looking.
It bulged bigger than a Steinway, gleamed
of high-lacquered black, and played everyone
like a mean thrill. All night we wore the masks
of chemical thieves. So children grew listless, so
the neighborhood dwindled
like a band of winter crickets. It was big,
we said, and made the measurements again.

Histories

Biological

Since before the concept of countries
and the wars that made them,
the world was working toward the couple.
It began with water; it began with light.
Then one cell divided but stayed clung
to its other half and would not let it
slip away. It was dark. They held
front to slippery back, overside to under.
They floated through the sea, trying
to think whether the lone moon
should envy them: each time
they decided *Yes*, another cell stayed.
They floated until they swam; they swam
until some stood and walked away
in pairs. Of course, they returned
to water for drink. Of course,
they followed it upstream. How else
would they have found others like them
who taught them how to sleep
warm under boughs and to fear
green snakes? Remember
those first two cells. Without
them, no him. No her. Don't leave, don't
go. The world's been so long waiting.

Biographical

When she was seven, he was already
the voice of milk filling a glass.
The world worked hard to bring them
to each other as the wind kept watch.
At thirteen, her body called out to him
with blood; seventeen, and the clothes
she dropped at the edge of sleep
seemed lessons in letting go
of some outer thing. Button and zipper,
snap and eyehook, each undoing
was the practice of a gift. Twenty, twenty-
five, then thirty so briefly—it was difficult
to wait; it took a long time: but who can doubt?
They didn't meet by accident even though
it goes like this: The dog fell
from the man's truck and was hit by the woman's.
Both pulled over, and to save them all
from the way the dog kicked, shuddered,
kicked, and frothed, the man took out his gun
and shot it. That dog she hit had ridden
through twelve years of back-truck wind
to reach that day. The man had to leave his house
early, cross four states, and then swerve
around a hole just to throw it there.

Historical

The powder of China's fireworks inspired
a different country to find a better way
to kill. The people of that country had a violence,
and that violence longed to take shape.
Each man carried this desire in his heart, aching there
against the membranes, expanding
into his blood until his insides coursed
with unrequited shape. He wanted to rid himself
of it, so sought to place it outside of him.
In trying, he filled his world
as he tried to get it right:
shape of catapult, that of powder packed
tight to the end of a gun, shape of ramrod,
then of oilcloth, shape of dynamite, bomb,
shape of beak, of talon, saber, tusk,
the edge of stone; of fist, of silvered ends of boots,
spurs, a whip— But no shape filled him
until he arrived again at his own hardness
and called it bullet. To hold one, smooth
and warming in his hands. Just right.

Ontological

What appeared as chance
is the god they are finding to thank
for the makers of those bullets that ended
the life of the dog, the makers of the gun
and barrel. But also
for the ones who made pavement, the road,
the truck, and their drivers. The couple
is thankful. They thank that god
for the hole that caused the swerve
that threw the dog, and then for the digger
who carved the ditch which held the three of them
inside its slope: dog, man, woman.
Imagine the precision of that god's timing,
their luck of it! They evolved into humans
who learned to drive and carry guns in cars.
The couple arrived right into
this god's plans exactly, exactly, as the sun
glinted off the windshields
and the dog rolled into the hollow made soft
by autumn undressing the last of her trees.

2.

Without Warning,
the Mist Came Down

The hill's peak is somewhere past
one more step away, and rising. Reaching
out cuts me from my hands.
Still higher, the flowers thin to spring's barest breath,

its least thought. When the rising ends,
I will lie among the few grasses.
There will be nowhere higher to go, until the bird
in the mist above me

calls out to the ground to declare its trees.

The Pardon

The man I was learning to live with
couldn't wait to finish the kitchen's yellow coat
before turning his brush on me.
If I'd known how soap and turpentine would turn
my skin raw against his hands,
I wouldn't have let him lean me back
across the floor. It took weeks

to heal and months to stop loving
the way mornings relaxed against the windows
trembled with light. Anything
was what I would have done to keep it bright
like that. But shoes, and spills . . .
The light grew careless and began to stumble in.

Later we did the kitchen blue, painting by night
to stay cool. We were almost done
when a moth fell to the floor, then struggled
toward the bare promise of a brightening window.
We tried to free it from the paint, but one wing
began to tear. It took nothing

to ruin that moth. The sun was making ready
to come in, tentative again, and slow.
The moth was awful with its broken self,
waiting for the light to take it. It took
nothing at all, gentle as we were.

This, Too, One Kind of Voice

After, I meant to cover the window
against the mountain lying brightly
under the moon. Where clouds passed over them,
bodies of dark hovered underneath, trembling
to separate light from lack. That trembling is one kind
of voice that asks never to be forsaken.
The egret in a pond of the mountain
asks this, too: she tips back her head
and calls out a sound like the length of her throat.
Nothing she can hear answers, but weeds
shiver on the banks.

Will There Be Police

when I die, and Sister Mark so proud
of the question. This,
in high school where our hands and mouths
held our first thoughts, and ideas
progressed from the Smoke Pit's back booth
where Kidder Diggs would one-hand me
from my underpants. Sister Mark wanted us to plan
our funerals to make us see the consequence
of all our living.
Most of the funerals turned into parties
with drinks in real glass and all the girls
in red. But I wanted cops. Twelve of them
at my trailer door like a bouquet of authority
and the walls coughing with their fists.
I wanted to hear the silence of crewcut men
with eyes tight as minnow flash.
One of them quiet as he shakes
my mini snow scenes and another's
ear so close to my heart he hears the last valve closing.
I wanted grief frightening as a sack
of white hair. I made it all up as I went along
with Kidder, his fingers fat as a scream.

Prodigy

When an animal wakes to find stolen
a seed that was to carry it across winter, it weighs its flesh

against the cold: balances moon hours to sun; bare branch
to bud; frost to breath. One might think such loss

a small thing, but the laws know better:
as how carbon gathers to itself until it is every living thing;

how matter is neither created nor destroyed. Sadness
is the velvet matter of the soul: it gets released; it goes somewhere.

We can prove it when we enter lakes and close our eyes
until we are elegant as vines. Then we can catch the grief

of animals. It enters without asking: the slow drying of snails,
the herons' sinking islands, chaff in the eye of a boar . . .

At night we can feel it most. Then we can place our hands
upon it: *Here*, and then, *here and here, and here.*

Asked Some 20 Questions, Many of Which Seem Like More Than One

What aspirations? Whose thighs? What does it
mean to dine upon fur? What was the intent?
Along which lines did you recline, and
what kind of fur? Who else, and with what logic? Was it
beautiful? Did it smell as if you were supposed to
back away? Why was it barricaded?
Which exit? Did the city face north or not north?
Does it burn at night? If it twitched, to what size
did it grow? Is there anything else? What did you
want to be? What does anyone mean by certain
precautions? Where are you supposed to be at each hour?
Which dream, and when did it explode? Who did your face?
Who held you there? Upon what type of broken glass?

Floating Even Now

I was to come up with the words I'd need
and practice them until they did not answer back.
But nothing I found held the raggedness
of light hunched against my window; no words together
spoke the sound of a bleeding tongue. I began
speaking of the pit of the mango, how furred and frightening
it is, how it is more than the words that find it, as are moths
who seek out their own burning.
Then there was how private and sullen
the eggplant is inside its skin. Of the four a.m. siren
which became the accident of my dreams.
As a way to make these things clear, I understand
I must speak of Laika,
the Russian dog who lived ten days alone in space as a test
and was then abandoned there.
Laika inside of Ursa, floating even now
where a star whose light we'll see for another eighty thousand years
may be collapsing, while here
each of the points on a buck is pointing to the next constellation,
formed on this day of the next possible word.

I'd Have Presented a Cup of Water or My Own Small Ax

She said she could read the dream
of anything, so they put her in a cage
overlooking, at first, the plum trees.

But they said this made it too easy,
that the fruit or the birds might be
where the visions were from.

So they put her underground,
and one woman dropped down
a handkerchief.

In the box, the woman
found the cloth's dream of waterfall,
released it up.

Then they sent down
a boy who had never woken,
but his dream was in a language

so large its edges hurt. The lemon
dreamt of chaff blowing over the field.
The shoes of rising spoons of heat.

When the people had nothing left
to send, they went home
and ate, some with their hands, some

very little. In the box, the woman grew
thinner. In her paleness, she shone
like a sail of the moon's own drift,

and so read that. Again and again,
as though it might release her.

Phantom Limb

1.

A scratch on my hand, a stunning illness,
and then waking from whiteness
into a room of the same: white sheets and white tile
and my arm gone,

2.

but messaging a code more Morse than pulse,
tapping a tattoo of arm into air.

3.

A god of empty spaces. Not the god
of what was, but the god of what was all along.

4.

In the mornings, I remember this absence by looking
at it. Absence is made
by emptiness, but is not emptiness.

5.

What the arm says is what space says.
Just last night I awoke as the moon filled the hand
then traced the shape of my face with its fingers.

Churn

The bear rose in my heart
but lay down again
because he thought it still winter.
Even as the buds were struggling to open their pink mouths
to say—

But their voices froze and fell into the dreams
of worms who uncurled themselves and began to eat.

Timing is like that.

The grasses of desire dream of my body's slow roll
back into them.

Now the blossoms are falling from their trees,
telling me I should look deep into them, past the faded blood
of their edges.

The redness there is a way to make it back, they say.

Analysis of the Moth

Why was the moth terrible?
Of course, it was my own heart, beating.

Why was the moth terrible?
At the window. I wanted it to be a face.

Why was the moth terrible?
Tell me your name. How you come at me and at me.

How should I come at you?
Like a mouth. Like a moth. Like blown hair.

How should you accept me?
Like a mouth. Like a buried twin.

How would you know me?
Your handprint is on my back.

How would I know you?
Your handprint is where I burn.

How did you feel this morning?
It beat at the window with ashy wings.

Why was the moth terrible?
It did not hold back the night.

Where was the night?
My face was pale inside of it, and burning.

As Walking Becomes
the Answer to the Road

The swifts diving back on their paths came to be
how I knew it was evening, time to keep walking
into the night until I became a tunnel
through to morning. The fallen twigs from the trees
told the wind's story of what came before
and what was to come. Somewhere along the way,
I remembered there was name for everything,
but nothing answered. They said, *Honey,*
it doesn't have to be this way, but the road
was already too clear with how far it could go.
So I pointed at the dogs with thin faces,
at the peonies blown into heaps, and the blue bus
of sky as it traveled overhead.

Seizure on the Siskyou Ridge

A dimming like the radio's pull
off the battery and then the drop into black ferns.
Body as medium—
cicadas drying their wings, pulse of an eel.

Lights flicker in the kitchens. The neck a conduit
of wide open fruit as the underself
goes absent as the ear's hidden coin, goes

full throttle to the gods, where no spoon in the mouth
can bring it back.

The cleaving and the cleaving.

While the body translates undersea tectonics
the body's inhabitant has flown into a nothing so wide it can speak
any tongue, ask any question, pay for answers
so dangerous they will not make

the long trip back. There, a row of knees on the ground
as one body awakens and its other falls back.
A spoon tucked into the sleeve while a woman says
There,

now, there. And then the mouth, its answer
dropped away and filling up with blood.

The Moss

is an artifact left by the voice of a god overtaken
by the steam of factories.
All day I sit with it, asking for things
absolute and unbroken.
Along a city's main street, people carry
themselves as if nothing
they hold can spill
as they board the trains. But
I am here, placing my head
against the sex-wet springiness of the moss,
listening for the furred voice of a forest, last call
of a god I can't remember how to love unless
it's with my body. The birds
don't mind. They don't wonder who left
the green, green voice to soften the arguments
of branches, the new rings expanding in each tree,
the homages to hunger
sung out by the barely feathered.

Plenty Comes at Night

Illusion of More:

Keep three good beers in the fridge,
but drink generic until company comes.
Share the good beer, then apologize
for running out. Someone
will buy more. They usually leave
at least three behind.

Driving:

All night around the same town
with the radio up. We knew
every song whole; they saved us
from the same conversation.

The Question:

We planned to steal our own car
for the insurance—just cross the state line
and leave it on a hillside. But first I wanted
to know how hard the cops would really work,
how fast we'd get the check.

Night Time:

We had a front door,
a path of worn carpet all the way
to the bathroom, a pile of shoes still hot
from double shift, and a bed
we fell into, still undressing.

Day Things:

We had two burners, a map, some plans,
and a sink. We'd fold the bed
so there was room to open the door.

The Car:

If it started, we'd joke, *Now we can go
anywhere.* Once, I stopped hard to miss a cat,
and a hubcap separated from the car
and spun from our sight
into the world of Beyond.

The Same Conversation:

When we had it, we weren't united
in wonder over the meaning of us.
We talked rent, the food
we stretched with oatmeal, the length
of work before another sleep.

Night:

Sleep, at least, was free, and so was talk
about how many ways we'd pull through.
Baby, I'd say, *let's do a garden.*
Baby, he'd say, *shh. Look at the moon*
through the curtain.

A Pileup, and Time, Besides

Whatever is given is best when given all at once, not
over time like time itself
or a tract of days so clear the sky forgets. I want it
pouring like air from a vacant building,
the windows gaped with atmosphere.

Everything happens in a moment, anyway. Let
someone else go back for the missing
ingredient. Meantime, I'll be eating
with my hands. I will be training myself
to walk upright with a stomach so crammed.
Why not?
        The timeline of history wrinkles, and we
disappear, along with ice ages and catheters,
wars and the invention of vinyl.

I do not want to wait: waiting is not patience, is
no more than hunger in beautiful clothing.
It feels urgent, how once we were cells, yet
a slip of heat wedged the night open
and then the world was suddenly full of us.

And now, here we are together,
and we wonder how it all came so far, like a back seat
in which the world happens quickly
because nobody's asking. The world, of course,
being first that cell and then an ocean coughing up
land and people,

and I call out, but a mouth has closed over mine
and I'm using a pair of pants as a pillow. Then the baby
is born and the house gets painted and somewhere
in the midst of all this a voice does or does not say
from the sky that it is good,

but we're recording it anyway, the way we see it
here, here with the windows rolled down,
wars going on, centuries of music spilling from the radio,
night and day streaming past, and the future
catalogued, but suddenly.

3.

I Wonder if I've
Told You Everything

Again the grass is telling me about myself, this time enlisting
the jays to use their voices to scratch the message
into the reams of sky.
Lie down

among us and stay, the blades say, offering fields
of themselves and telling me green.

Another line of ants carries melted stones of the sun
through the grass. Revealed is the owl
who keeps watch over movement,

over grass sway and grass ripple. Grass rises from the place
where day of body and day of grass overlap.

All of it in me, I ask, *is the promise?* The grass answers, *Yes*.
Answers, *Do not keep us from ourself within you*.

I feel how my heart can go green and bladed.
I have always missed the mouths of grazing things.

North

Yes, it said, and I heard it. Followed
whatever looked like it would take me
north, needed to go that far into the cold. But no
trail took me there enough, so I issued voice
in its direction, waiting to be asked again. I sang
from within the shadow of a mountain, the shadow stretching
long as a town in which everyone wants
what's behind the glass.

The shadow accepted what I gave, began to steal
from the little light remaining to make more room
for what I offered. No one told me
I was alone and singing to a growing darkness
in which no dark bird preened, no bird
called out a tether to the light.

The Allocations of Sound

When deafness begins, birds
become more important. First the warblers fade,

opening the sky
by the space of their notes. Waking up, it is difficult

to tell
exactly how much of the night will not leave your ears.

The birds continue to disappear, trailing off like the sky's
ellipses.

The crane is nearly equal to a warning of seven longspurs.
A raven, thirty redwings, lifting.

Even the voices of the geese are so dim they throw
no shadow across the corridors of sound. But

no birds come forward to carry that voice into open, bronze
and bare as a throat thrown back.

Admission

Out here my body has grown savage as teeth
and cautious as fur against the sky and grasses.
The city I try to remember is the sound
of a man forever descending the pit of trains
and a voice hungry as a spoon.
I meant to be good at all this wildness—
its sky of harvest promises
and the pears falling from their trees
so the ground can start them over.
But the trees are too far outside of me;
the animals scratching into the walls
speak in a language of no certain city.
I meant to unlearn buildings
and their slants against light. To find
the river's drift in the spine
and the cabbage tightness of the throat
during the tumult of rain. I sought words
of the vein and the slow pull of sap, of hair
rising at the nape. Out here, the moon flashes
from the eyes of the hungry. Every outer thing
has a voice, and none of it is human.

Gravity

The cliff's drop was a dare
of physics: sheer, cut inward,
and final

into the water below.
I lay at the edge to find the place
within me most connected to dying
that day. Whichever part went heaviest

was how to know. Then a slight skin rose
on the water's surface. A swelling and
then smooth again.

The wind rushed
over my back and died, tamed by openness.
The stones I dropped into the water
made no sound at all.

Counting on Your Presence

We enter the water by the thousands,
the threads of our clothing darkening
into water, into the evening that hangs
at the edge of shore.

We are not allowed to touch.
We are not allowed to ask when.
Each of us is a hallway between worlds.

Daylight clings to our lips and hair
and lingers at what shines back. Eventually,
the light pale as a rope appears
only when we close our eyes.

We use what we can of such light,
but even that dwindles, so we use the dwindling
to interpret the answers of how much longer.

The water in the roots of trees.
The waves that rise and fall without asking.
The dark mouths around us—

if they begin to disappear, we will have to wait
until morning or new light to be sure.

The Lost Man

No one found the man in the tree, though
he waited. He had to find himself,
then climb down, thin, nearly green

as the water from which he'd pulled himself.
Understand, he had no tongue. Understand,

he could not write. This is about a story
he did not tell and which was never learned.

When he made a frame with his hands,
the spider understood it was empty, but
went no further. When he cut a pocket
from its shirt, the cat could see
the hole meant something, and went no further.

He found a letter on the street. Its words
understood they could be anything,
so were silent, and he knew what they meant by this.

Many things were in the kingdom of this man, but
he was alive, so suffering was and was not among them.

When he breathed from the air, he was careful
to put back what he took.

The Air Anniversary

As the jays ratchet up the heat of the morning,
the breeze searches someplace cooler. In the field, heat separates
the stalks of wheat,
                     does it thoroughly, until every chaff
is an isolate of light: clear-bodied and independent.

Air vibrates the backs of cicadas, wends its way through a rattle
of branches, and pools in the roots of paling grasses.

It enters cradles at the centers of trees, issues
from the shadowed mouths, settles within the promise
of leaves, leaning from the arms of what is pitched with shade.

Air in the branches of what is dead and what is
living. Air as the final shape
of what has disappeared:
                  the leaf's fill stripped from its veins,
              the shadow shifted east from west,
                   pages blown from the table, and the light
                      faded from days laid open as a sky.

Air as what eternally is, like any word spoken: what appears

      first as voice is filled by air. When it goes
silent, is filled with air again.

Laying Them Down, Telling Them Rest

In my sleep, the dead show me
that it hurts. More than I thought,
and in places I hadn't considered.

It hurts in the willows, where I am
to notch the branches once, once

for each of them.
Leaves grow like cool tongues
from the slashings. And it hurts

in the field of cut grass,
which grows again but is never saved.

At the edge of the field
is the Tree of Flashed Faces, and from this hangs
a mirror. I am to cross the field in its golden height

and count the scratches of wheat on my arms
because they say it hurts there, too.

The Moss Breathes Back

When the grouse startled from the brush, the moss.

When stone fell against stone and broke
open, the moss.

The moss when hoof sparked against the trail
and at the screech just before the owl into rabbit.

Water against water, the moss.

The winter branch cracked away in its hollow groan.

Time across grasses is faster than for the moss.

With my head softened by it, I hear the hoof,
the feather, and the stone. *I hear you*, I say.

And later, *I hear you*, the moss breathes back
to the shadows of leaves.

Fly Tier's Monomania

If one bait is unsuccessful, change to another.
–THE SAS SURVIVAL HANDBOOK

I. The Dark Heart

My dog's fur shone in his fever,
and I clipped all I could.
On the floor in the dark,
I counted his breaths, whispered
how he was my Kansas, my little
undertaker, the dropped anchor of sleep.
I meant to eat by the flies
of his fur, so named them for
the black realm of my heart
where he lives. My biter
of children. Scar of my palm.

II. The Last Word

I dedicate this fly to the fish
of the fallen river. It is a poem
of hook and shank and feather.
It sinks like a bone, casts
like the logic of knives.
The song of my own hair, it is
how I call them from their stones.

III. The Strangler

Black as a mouth
of water and laid over
in a silver rib, the fly is
so tight
the hook
is a grace. I dreamed it
as the hunger of fish.
I cast it as the hunger
of flesh.

IV. The Voyeur

I want your hair and the feather
of what has fallen. Give me
the sweepings of barbers, the heads
of strangers who leave
their curtains open as a wing.
I want a lock to call you by, I want
to tie you into my crescent of hunger.
I mean to take you home.

Tomorrow, Tomorrow

One tree sometimes makes another tree.
–GERTRUDE STEIN

And one bird sometimes makes another, until
the sky is shadowed in the peeled-off flights
of black bodies wing-lit and foreign
in their escapes past us. In a house
at the mouth of the Salmon River, I wake
to a night sealed in by clouds, but brightened
by winter. The river hauls itself to the sea.
The water is darkest where bundles
of weed-wrapped sticks pass and shadow, so many
the banks should be scoured by morning.
But even then, it is the same as with each night:
the sticks, the river, the sea.
Sticks bound into long bodies float past.
They skim lightly, but are never coming back.

The Speaking

I cannot locate the fire: at night
I know it is there because of the smoke and singe.
By day, it speaks to my throat

and I answer but can't remember.
Every tree holds a knot, a tight bloom
against its years. It answers to the place
where you were known by somebody
who carried you against his chest. I can tell

when someone has accepted fire
by the sudden vanity of another tree,
by the way it allows itself as mirror to what burns.

I go to the trees after storms;
I listen. I must find the one that is to be kindled
with what I would be kindled by. I must find it

before it ignites without me and the birds are ruined,
before the air is pulled from the lungs of the forest.
Oh, forest, among you, I trust there is a speaking.

What the Stones Allow

The rocks: brown and furred
from the shaken arms of pines,
leaving me wanting to peel off their skin
and find their stone hearts, their stone
tongues pressed down with what words
the throat could not give up. In a tree

there is bark and there is underbark, matter
soft and green as the eye opening
to the belly of light at the edge of the world.
And the rabbit

is many parts of rabbit:
the slide of guts and the veins in the ears
that give back the heat of deserts.
Layer after next, the rabbit is bone and tooth,
is fur and skin and fat. Muscle stretched
like the highways of the still standing.

But a stone is only body. A brute of shape
left by the ice age that is never coming back
to claim it. All of them live

so far past the first tree. Yes, they would allow me
to warm myself on them in the mornings.
There's nothing else I can take
from them, so complete is their hulk.
This one is splitting sharply down
the middle. This one's crying out for milk

or blood. They are not gentle. They do not
mean to be.

The Brittingham Prize in Poetry

Ronald Wallace | GENERAL EDITOR

And Her Soul Out of Nothing | Olena Kalytiak Davis
Rita Dove, Judge, 1997

Bardo | Suzanne Paola
Donald Hall, Judge, 1998

A Field Guide to the Heavens | Frank X. Gaspar
Robert Bly, Judge, 1999

A Path between Houses | Greg Rappleye
Alicia Ostricker, Judge, 2000

Horizon Note | Robin Behn
Mark Doty, Judge, 2001

Acts of Contortion | Anna George Meek
Edward Hirsch | Judge, 2002

The Room Where I Was Born | Brian Teare
Kelly Cherry, Judge, 2003

Sea of Faith | John Brehm
Carl Dennis, Judge, 2004

Jagged with Love | Susanna Childress
Billy Collins, Judge, 2005

New Jersey | Betsy Andrews
Linda Gregerson, Judge, 2007

Meditations on Rising and Falling | Philip Pardi
David St. John, Judge, 2008

Bird Skin Coat | Angela Sorby
Marilyn Nelson, Judge, 2009

The Mouths of Grazing Things | Jennifer Boyden
Robert Pinsky, Judge, 2010